Small Business Success: Strategies for Sustainable Growth

Table of contents

A. Sustainable Practices and Social Responsibility

B. Exit Strategies and Succession Planning

C. Ensuring a Lasting Legacy

Introduction

In the world of business, small is no longer synonymous with insignificant. Small businesses are the lifeblood of economies, the incubators of innovation, and the cornerstones of communities. Their impact reaches far beyond their size, and their success stories are woven into the fabric of our modern entrepreneurial landscape.

This eBook, "Small Business Success: Strategies for Sustainable Growth," is your guide to unlocking the full potential of your small business. Whether you're just starting your entrepreneurial journey or have been at the helm for years, our aim is to provide you with the knowledge, strategies, and inspiration needed to not only survive but to thrive in the ever-evolving business world.

We will delve into a multitude of aspects crucial to your small business's success, all through the lens of sustainable growth. This includes understanding the metrics that truly matter, building a robust foundation, crafting an impactful brand identity, and acquiring and retaining loyal customers.

Financial management and planning will become your allies as you learn to navigate the choppy waters of cash flow, investments, and capital. And when the time is right, we'll help you explore the paths to scale your small business wisely and responsibly.

Amid the ever-changing business landscape, adaptability and innovation will be your secret weapons. This eBook will arm you with the tools and insights to stay competitive and agile.

But it's not just about the business itself; it's also about the people who drive it. We'll dive into the art of leadership and team-building, exploring how to nurture a high-performing team that shares your vision.

Every small business faces challenges, but your ability to overcome them will set you apart. We'll share stories of resilience and success, alongside strategies to weather the storms.

Ultimately, our goal is to help you plan for the long-term sustainability of your business. From sustainable practices to succession planning, we'll explore how to ensure your business leaves a lasting legacy.

This eBook is more than just words on a screen; it's a roadmap for your small business journey. As you navigate through its pages, you'll find actionable advice, real-life examples, and a wealth of resources to draw from.

Chapter 1

Defining Small Business Success

In the world of small businesses, success is a multifaceted concept. It's more than just financial profit; it encompasses a holistic blend of achievements that not only ensure survival but pave the path for sustainable growth. In this chapter, we'll explore what success truly means for small businesses, the key metrics you need to measure it, and the indispensable role of vision and mission.

A. What Success Means for Small Businesses

Small businesses are the beating heart of entrepreneurship, and their success is a reflection of the dreams, aspirations, and hard work of their founders. Success for a small business can be boiled down to a few fundamental components:

Financial Health: This is perhaps the most apparent facet of success. It involves making a profit, managing expenses effectively, and achieving financial stability. It's the ability to reinvest in the business and provide a return to stakeholders.

Customer Satisfaction: Happy customers are the cornerstone of a thriving small business. Success means delivering exceptional products or services and fostering lasting relationships with your clientele.

Employee Fulfillment: Your team is an essential part of your success. It involves providing a positive work environment, growth opportunities, and job satisfaction for your employees.

Community Impact: Small businesses have a unique opportunity to make a difference in their local communities. Success includes contributing positively to the community through job creation, ethical practices, and community involvement.

Innovation and Adaptability: Being successful means not just achieving a momentary win but continually evolving and staying relevant. It's about innovation, adaptation, and staying ahead of the competition.

B. Key Metrics for Measuring Success

To measure your small business's success effectively, you must rely on specific metrics that align with your goals and ambitions. Here are some key performance indicators (KPIs) to consider:

Revenue Growth: Track the increase in your business's revenue over time to ensure you're growing.

Profit Margin: It's not just about revenue but also about how efficiently you convert revenue into profit.

Customer Acquisition and Retention: Measure your ability to attract and retain customers.

Cash Flow: Monitoring your cash flow is vital to ensure you can cover expenses and invest in growth.

Customer Satisfaction and Loyalty: Consider metrics like Net Promoter

Score (NPS) to gauge customer satisfaction and loyalty.

Employee Turnover Rate: A high turnover rate can indicate problems in your workplace culture.

C. The Role of Vision and Mission

Your small business's vision and mission are the compass that guides your journey. A clear vision sets the long-term direction, while the mission outlines your purpose and the means to achieve that vision.

Well-defined vision and mission:

Inspire: They inspire you, your team, and your customers. They provide a sense of purpose and direction.

Align: They align all activities within your business, ensuring that everyone is working toward the same goals.

Differentiate: They differentiate your business from competitors. They define what makes your small business unique.

Adapt: They provide a stable foundation while allowing flexibility to adapt to changing market conditions.

Measure: They serve as a measuring stick for success. Your actions and results should reflect your vision and mission.

As we journey through this eBook, keep these fundamental concepts of success in mind. Success for your small business may involve reaching financial milestones, creating lasting customer relationships, or leaving a positive impact on your community. Ultimately, it's about balancing these aspects and aligning them with your vision and mission. With this foundation, you'll be better equipped to explore the strategies for sustainable growth that we'll delve into in the chapters to come.

Chapter 2

Building a Strong Foundation

In the world of small business, just as in construction, the strength of your foundation determines the resilience and longevity of your venture. This chapter is dedicated to helping you lay the groundwork for your small business's success. We'll explore three essential components that form the bedrock of your enterprise:

A. Business Planning and Strategy

The Blueprint of Success: Business planning is the blueprint for your small business. It's not just a one-time activity but an ongoing process that evolves with your business. A well-thought-out business plan should encompass:

A clear vision and mission statement.

Defined short-term and long-term goals.

Strategies for achieving those goals.

Market analysis and competition assessment.

Financial projections and budgeting.

Strategic Thinking: Your business strategy is your roadmap for achieving your goals. It's about making informed decisions, setting priorities, and adapting to changes. Effective business strategy considers:

Target market and audience.

Competitive positioning.

Pricing and revenue models.

Marketing and sales strategies.

Risk management and contingency planning.

Measuring Progress: Establish key performance indicators (KPIs) to track your progress and adapt your strategies as needed. Regularly revisit and adjust your business plan and strategy to stay aligned with your goals.

B. Legal and Financial Considerations

Legal Structure: Choosing the right legal structure for your small business is crucial. Consider options such as sole proprietorship, partnership, LLC, or corporation. Each has its advantages and disadvantages in terms of liability, taxation, and management.

Regulatory Compliance: Be aware of the legal and regulatory requirements that apply to your industry and location. This includes permits, licenses, taxes, and employment laws. Compliance helps you avoid costly legal issues.

Financial Management: Effective financial management is a cornerstone of a strong foundation. This involves:

Creating a realistic budget.

Monitoring cash flow to ensure you can cover expenses.

Proper bookkeeping and accounting practices.

Planning for taxes and ensuring financial transparency.

Funding Options: Explore different sources of funding for your business, such as personal savings, loans, investors, or crowdfunding. Each has its advantages and considerations that can impact your business's financial health.

C. Finding Your Niche

Understanding Niche Markets: Finding your niche means identifying a specific, well-defined target market or audience for your products or services. This is often more effective than trying to appeal to a broad and diverse audience.

Market Research: Conduct thorough market research to understand your niche's needs, preferences, and pain points. This research helps you tailor your offerings to meet their specific demands.

Competitive Analysis: Analyze your competitors in the niche market. Identify gaps in their offerings and opportunities for differentiation. What can you do better or differently?

Value Proposition: Define your unique value proposition. How does your small business solve problems or fulfill needs in a way that sets you apart from others in your niche?

Niche Marketing Strategies: Craft marketing campaigns and strategies tailored to your niche audience. This personalization is more likely to resonate and generate interest and loyalty.

As you work on these elements, remember that building a strong foundation for your small business is an ongoing process. It requires adaptability and a keen understanding of your market, legal requirements, and your own business's strengths and weaknesses. With a robust foundation in place, you'll be better prepared to embark on the journey towards sustainable growth and success.

Chapter 3

Marketing and Branding

In the bustling landscape of small business, the twin engines of marketing and branding propel your venture forward. This chapter explores three pivotal aspects that will help you reach and resonate with your target audience:

A. Crafting a Compelling Brand Identity

The Essence of Branding: Your brand is not just a logo or a name; it's the essence of your business. Crafting a compelling brand identity involves defining what your business represents, what it promises, and how it stands apart in the market.

Brand Elements: Develop consistent brand elements, including your logo, color palette, typography, and tone of voice. These elements should convey your brand's personality and values.

Value Proposition: Your brand's value proposition should be clear. What unique benefits do you offer to your customers, and why should they choose your small business over others?

Customer-Centric Approach: Understand your target audience deeply. Your brand should resonate with their needs, preferences, and aspirations.

Brand Consistency: Maintain consistency across all brand touchpoints, from your website and social media profiles to your product packaging. Consistency builds trust and recognition.

B. Digital Marketing Strategies

Online Presence: Establishing a robust online presence is vital. Your website is often the first point of contact for potential customers. Ensure it's user-friendly, informative, and visually appealing.

Search Engine Optimization (SEO): Optimize your website and content for search engines. This helps improve your visibility in search results and drives organic traffic.

Content Marketing: Create valuable, relevant content that educates, entertains, or solves problems for your target audience. Blog posts, videos, infographics, and podcasts are all avenues for content.

Social Media Marketing: Leverage social media platforms to engage with your audience, build brand awareness, and promote your products or services.

Email Marketing: A well-crafted email marketing strategy can help nurture leads, retain customers, and generate sales. Personalization and segmentation are key here.

Paid Advertising: Consider paid advertising through platforms like Google Ads or social media advertising. These can be effective for reaching a broader audience or targeting specific demographics.

C. Traditional Marketing Approaches

Print Media: Traditional print media like brochures, flyers, and business cards can still be effective, particularly in local markets.

Networking: Face-to-face interactions through networking events, trade shows, or local business organizations can help you build relationships and gain exposure.

Direct Mail: Targeted direct mail campaigns can yield results, especially when aiming to reach a local or specific demographic.

Referral Marketing: Encourage your satisfied customers to refer others to your business. Word-of-mouth marketing is a powerful tool.

Public Relations: Develop a public relations strategy to create a positive image for your small business. Media coverage, press releases, and community involvement can all contribute to your brand's reputation.

Community Involvement: Participating in local events, sponsorships, or charity work can help create a positive brand image and connect with your community.

Remember, the most effective marketing strategies are those that align with your target audience, budget, and overall business goals. It's not about choosing between digital and traditional marketing but finding the right mix for your specific small business. Craft a brand identity that resonates with your audience, harness the power of digital and traditional marketing, and you'll be well on your way to sustainable growth and success.

Chapter 4

Customer Acquisition and Retention

In the world of small business, acquiring and retaining customers is the lifeblood of success. This chapter explores the essential elements that form the cornerstone of customer-centric strategies:

A. Understanding Your Target Audience

The Importance of Knowing Your **Audience:** Understanding your target audience is the first step in building meaningful connections and delivering products or services that truly meet their needs.

Buyer Personas: Create detailed buyer personas that represent your ideal customers. These should include demographic information, behaviors, pain points, and preferences.

Market Research: Conduct thorough market research to uncover trends, consumer behavior, and competitor strategies. This knowledge provides insights to tailor your offerings effectively.

Segmentation: Divide your audience into segments based on common characteristics. This allows for more personalized marketing and product/service offerings.

Feedback and Communication: Actively engage with your audience through surveys, feedback forms, and social media. Encourage open communication to gain insights into their evolving needs and preferences.

B. Sales and Customer Relationship Management

Effective Sales Strategies: Develop sales strategies that align with your customer base. This includes setting clear sales targets, training your sales team, and defining a sales process.

Customer Relationship Management (CRM): Implement a CRM system to manage customer interactions and track valuable data. This helps in personalizing customer experiences and improving retention.

Sales Funnel: Understand the sales funnel stages - from awareness to conversion - and tailor your strategies to guide customers smoothly through this journey.

Customer Support: Exceptional customer support is crucial. Be responsive, helpful, and empathetic to customer needs, whether it's answering questions, addressing concerns, or providing post-purchase assistance.

Feedback Loops: Create feedback loops to gather information about customer experiences. Analyze this feedback to continuously improve your products, services, and customer interactions.

C. Customer Loyalty and Retention Strategies

Building Loyalty: Customer loyalty is earned through consistent, high-quality experiences. Consider loyalty programs, discounts, and exclusive offers to reward repeat customers.

Personalization: Tailor your communications and offers to individual customers based on their past interactions and preferences. Personalized experiences create a sense of value and connection.

Surprise and Delight: Occasionally, surprise your customers with unexpected gestures, whether it's a thank-you note, a small gift, or exclusive access to new products.

Customer Feedback Integration: Act on customer feedback by making improvements that address their concerns or desires. Show that you're responsive to their needs.

Retention Campaigns: Implement retention marketing campaigns, such as email newsletters, to stay connected with past customers and provide them with valuable content and offers.

Continuous Engagement: Regularly engage with your customers through social media, email marketing, and other channels. Share your business journey, provide insights, and encourage them to be part of your story.

Acquiring and retaining customers is an ongoing journey that requires commitment and adaptability. By understanding your audience, implementing effective sales and customer relationship management strategies, and investing in customer loyalty and retention efforts, your small business can not only attract customers but build lasting relationships that fuel sustainable growth and success.

Chapter 5

Financial Management

In the world of small business, the backbone of success lies in effective financial management. This chapter explores key financial considerations, offering guidance to secure your business's fiscal health and drive sustainable growth.

A. Budgeting and Financial Planning

The Power of Budgeting: A well-crafted budget is a roadmap for your financial journey. It helps you allocate resources, set financial goals, and stay on track. Key components of budgeting include:

Revenue projections

Expense management

Contingency funds

Investment planning

Setting Financial Goals: Clearly define your financial goals, both short-term and long-term. Goals act as motivation and direction, guiding your budgeting and financial planning efforts.

Regular Monitoring: A budget is not static; it's a dynamic tool that requires regular monitoring and adjustments. Track your financial performance against your budget to ensure you're meeting your goals.

Emergency Funds: Always set aside emergency funds to handle unexpected expenses or economic downturns. This provides a safety net for your business's financial stability.

B. Managing Cash Flow

Cash Flow Management: Managing cash flow is fundamental for small business survival. This involves understanding when and where money enters and exits your business. Strategies include:

Monitoring accounts receivable and payable

Efficient inventory management

Negotiating favorable payment terms with suppliers

Short-Term Financing: Consider short-term financing options, such as a line of credit or business credit card, to cover temporary cash flow gaps. Ensure you have a plan to pay off these loans promptly.

Forecasting Cash Flow: Create cash flow forecasts to anticipate potential financial challenges. This enables you to take proactive measures and avoid cash flow crises.

Reducing Overhead Costs: Identify areas where you can reduce overhead costs without sacrificing quality or customer service. Cutting unnecessary expenses can significantly impact cash flow.

C. Investment and Growth Capital

Investment Strategies: Identify opportunities for investment that align with your business's growth goals. This might include investing in new technology, equipment, marketing campaigns, or personnel.

Debt vs. Equity Financing: Evaluate whether debt or equity financing is more suitable for your business. Debt financing involves loans, while equity financing means selling a share of your business to investors.

Venture Capital and Angel Investors: Explore the possibility of raising capital through venture capitalists or angel investors if your business has high-growth potential. This often requires a well-prepared business plan and a compelling pitch.

Bootstrapping: If external funding isn't immediately accessible, consider bootstrapping your business by reinvesting profits. This approach can offer full control and independence but may limit growth speed.

Grants and Subsidies: Investigate government grants, subsidies, or industry-specific programs that may provide financial support to small businesses.

Remember, the key to financial management is not just to balance the books but to leverage your financial resources strategically. By budgeting effectively, managing cash flow, and making wise decisions regarding investment and growth capital, your small business can establish a solid financial foundation for long-term success and growth.

Chapter 6

Scaling Your Small Business

As your small business thrives, the idea of scaling becomes a tantalizing prospect. This chapter ventures into the strategies and considerations for scaling your business effectively:

A. Expanding Your Product/Service Offerings

Diversifying Offerings: Expanding your product or service offerings can breathe new life into your business. This may involve:

Introducing complementary products or services.

Developing variations or premium versions of existing offerings.

Identifying gaps in the market and filling them with innovative solutions.

Customer Needs: Keep a close eye on changing customer needs and market trends. Your expansion should align with these evolving demands.

Market Research: In-depth market research is essential before introducing new products or services. Understand your target audience, competition, and potential challenges.

Testing and Feedback: Pilot new offerings with a select group of customers and gather feedback. This data helps you refine your offerings before a full-scale launch.

B. Geographic and Market Expansion

Local and Regional Expansion: Consider expanding your business's reach to adjacent regions or localities. Understand the nuances of these markets, including customer preferences, competition, and regulatory requirements.

Global Market Entry: If your business has ambitions to go global, conduct thorough market research on international markets. Evaluate the cultural, legal, and economic factors that may impact your expansion.

Online Presence: The internet offers opportunities for worldwide reach. Leverage e-commerce and digital marketing to tap into broader markets without the need for physical presence.

Franchising or Licensing: Explore the option of franchising your business or licensing your intellectual property to expand your brand's presence in new locations.

C. Strategic Partnerships

Collaborations: Building strategic partnerships can help your business access new markets, technologies, or customer bases. Consider collaborations with complementary businesses in your industry.

Joint Ventures: Joint ventures involve shared ownership of a new entity for a specific project or market entry. These partnerships can provide resources and expertise beyond your current capabilities.

Distribution Partnerships: Partner with distributors or retailers to expand your product's reach. This is especially effective for consumer goods and retail businesses.

Technology Alliances: Forge alliances with technology companies to enhance your business's capabilities. This can be beneficial for tech startups and businesses seeking innovation.

Mergers and Acquisitions: In some cases, acquiring or merging with another company may be the most effective way to scale rapidly. These endeavors require comprehensive due diligence and a clear integration strategy.

Scaling your small business is an exciting journey, but it comes with its share of challenges. As you contemplate expanding your product or service offerings, entering new markets, or forming strategic partnerships, remember the importance of research, planning, and adaptability. Scaling should be a well-thought-out process that aligns with your long-term vision for sustainable growth and continued success.

Chapter 8

Leadership and Team Building

In the realm of small business, effective leadership and a high-performing team can be the difference between mediocrity and excellence. This chapter delves into the essential aspects of cultivating leadership skills, nurturing strong teams, and prioritizing employee development and satisfaction:

A. Effective Leadership Skills

Vision and Communication: Effective leaders have a clear vision and communicate it persuasively. They inspire and align their team by painting a compelling picture of the future.

Decision-Making: Leaders make informed, timely decisions. They weigh options, consider the consequences, and take action confidently. They're not afraid to take calculated risks.

Empathy and Emotional Intelligence: Leaders understand and empathize with their team members. They have high emotional intelligence, enabling them to navigate complex interpersonal relationships.

Adaptability: Effective leaders can adapt to changing circumstances and unexpected challenges. They are flexible and encourage their team to embrace change.

Delegation: Delegation is crucial for leaders. Effective leaders know when to empower their team members to take ownership of tasks, allowing them to develop and grow.

B. Building and Managing a High-Performing Team

Recruitment and Onboarding: Building a high-performing team starts with recruiting the right talent. Create a thorough and inclusive onboarding process to integrate new team members effectively.

Clear Roles and Responsibilities: Define clear roles and responsibilities for each team member. This reduces confusion and helps everyone understand their contributions to the team's success.

Team Building Activities: Plan team-building activities to foster trust and camaraderie. A cohesive team is more likely to collaborate effectively and perform at a high level.

Regular Feedback: Implement regular performance feedback and evaluation processes. Acknowledge achievements and address areas for improvement.

Conflict Resolution: Address conflicts within the team promptly and constructively. An effective leader acts as a mediator to maintain a harmonious working environment.

C. Employee Development and Satisfaction

Training and Development: Invest in the training and development of your employees. Continuous learning keeps your team's skills up to date and boosts job satisfaction.

Recognition and Rewards: Recognize and reward exceptional performance. This can be in the form of monetary incentives, promotions, or simply words of appreciation.

Work-Life Balance: Support work-life balance for your team members. Encourage flexible work arrangements and time off to maintain their well-being.

Employee Engagement: Keep your team engaged and motivated by involving them in decision-making and providing opportunities for them to contribute to the company's success.

Feedback Loops: Create feedback loops that allow employees to voice their concerns and suggestions. Act on this feedback to improve the work environment.

Effective leadership, strong team dynamics, and employee development and satisfaction are interconnected. They form a harmonious trifecta that drives your small business towards success. By honing your leadership skills, building a high-performing team, and prioritizing employee well-being, you create a positive and productive work culture that fuels sustainable growth and prosperity.

Chapter 9

Overcoming Challenges and Obstacles

In the pursuit of small business success, challenges and obstacles are inevitable. This chapter explores the common challenges faced by small businesses, strategies for resilience, and inspiring success stories that have surmounted adversity:

A. Common Challenges Faced by Small Businesses

Financial Strain: Limited capital, cash flow fluctuations, and access to funding can pose significant financial challenges.

Competition: Small businesses often operate in saturated markets, making it challenging to stand out and gain market share.

Regulatory Compliance: Navigating complex regulations and compliance issues can be a barrier, especially in highly regulated industries.

Marketing and Visibility: Attracting and retaining customers in a competitive landscape is a persistent challenge.

Talent Acquisition: Recruiting and retaining skilled employees can be difficult for small businesses competing with larger corporations.

Risk Management: Small businesses often have limited resources for risk management and disaster recovery planning.

Adaptation to Change: The ability to adapt to rapidly changing technology and consumer behavior is a continuous challenge.

B. Strategies for Resilience

Effective Planning: Develop a robust business plan that accounts for potential challenges and provides strategies for mitigation.

Financial Prudence: Maintain healthy financial practices, including prudent budgeting and cash flow management.

Leverage Technology: Embrace technology and automation to streamline operations and improve efficiency.

Networking and Collaboration: Build strong relationships with peers and mentors to gain insights and support during challenging times.

Adaptability: Be open to change and proactively adapt to market shifts and consumer trends.

Diversification: Diversify your product or service offerings to reduce dependency on a single revenue stream.

Customer-Centric Approach: Prioritize customer satisfaction and loyalty to weather competitive storms.

Chapter 10

Planning for Long-Term Sustainability

Sustainable growth is the pinnacle of small business success. This chapter explores the strategies to ensure your small business not only prospers but leaves a lasting legacy for future generations:

A. Sustainable Practices and Social Responsibility

Environmental Sustainability: Adopt eco-friendly practices to minimize your environmental footprint. This can include energy-efficient operations, waste reduction, and responsible sourcing.

Community Involvement: Engage with your local community through philanthropy, volunteering, or partnerships. Contributing positively to your community builds goodwill and long-term relationships.

Ethical Business Practices: Uphold ethical standards in all aspects of your business, from supply chain management to employee relations. Ethical businesses tend to enjoy lasting trust and customer loyalty.

Diversity and Inclusion: Foster a diverse and inclusive workplace. Embracing different perspectives not only enriches your organization but resonates positively with customers.

Corporate Social Responsibility (CSR): Develop a CSR strategy that aligns with your values and addresses social issues. This can include supporting charitable causes, promoting sustainability, and practicing fair labor standards.

B. Exit Strategies and Succession Planning

Succession Planning: Create a succession plan to ensure the smooth transition of leadership and management when the time comes. Identify potential successors, provide training, and document key processes.

Exit Strategies: Explore exit strategies, whether it's selling your business, passing it on to family, merging, or even closing. Having an exit plan is crucial for securing the legacy of your business.

Legal and Financial Consultation: Seek legal and financial guidance to structure your exit in the most tax-efficient and financially secure manner.

Timing Considerations: Timing is crucial in exit planning. Knowing when to exit is often as important as how to exit.

C. Ensuring a Lasting Legacy

Documenting Your Story: Record the history and evolution of your business. Create a written or visual narrative that highlights your journey, values, and milestones.

Mentoring and Knowledge Transfer: Mentor the next generation of leaders in your business. Share your knowledge, experiences, and insights to ensure continuity.

Brand Preservation: Maintain the integrity of your brand and reputation. Your brand's image and values should transcend transitions.

Maintaining Relationships: Foster lasting relationships with customers, employees, and business partners. Trust and loyalty are integral to building a lasting legacy.

Philanthropy and Endowments: Consider creating charitable foundations or endowments tied to your business to perpetuate your impact and legacy in your community.

Planning for long-term sustainability is not just about business growth but about creating a legacy that endures. By embracing sustainable practices, social responsibility, devising thoughtful exit strategies, and nurturing the principles that matter most to your business, you can ensure that your small business leaves a lasting mark on the world and continues to thrive well into the future.